The Whited Air:
Mary Paul in Winter

poems by

Susie Paul

Finishing Line Press
Georgetown, Kentucky

The Whited Air:
Mary Paul in Winter

Copyright © 2021 by Susie Paul
ISBN 978-1-64662-636-6 First Edition
All rights reserved under International and Pan-American Copyright Conventions. No part of this book may be reproduced in any manner whatsoever without written permission from the publisher, except in the case of brief quotations embodied in critical articles and reviews.

ACKNOWLEDGMENTS

I am grateful to the Vermont Historical Society for sharing their transcripts of the letters of Mary Stiles Paul to her father Bela Paul, as well as other papers related to her family.

Thank you to Jodi and Eileen for allowing me to stay with them in Boston and guiding me to and through Lowell, MA, where this collection is set. Many people have encouraged me in this work, which has been a long time in the making and the finding of a home. Thank you Jeanie, Bart, Mike, and Barbara. Thank you Gene and Liz for the photographs, Alisa for the gorgeous paintings. Thank you Andrew and Katherine for the gift of your understanding. Mrs. Brown, I wish you were here to see that I have at last come through.

Thank you Amelia and Joseph for reflecting my creative urges, and your dad's, in your own. Finally, thank you Mama, Helen Paul, for all that you taught me and continue to teach me about persistence and resilience in the face of all matter of challenges.

Publisher: Leah Huete de Maines
Editor: Christen Kincaid
Cover Art: Alisa Koch
Author Photo: Liz Tucker
Cover Design: Elizabeth Maines McCleavy

Order online: www.finishinglinepress.com
also available on amazon.com

Author inquiries and mail orders:
Finishing Line Press
PO Box 1626
Georgetown, Kentucky 40324
USA

Table of Contents

Introduction 1

Rhyme 2

Counting 3

What I Want 4

Hens 5

Shoes 6

Lace 7

The Bells 8

Somnambulism 9

Touch 10

Peddlers 11

At the Lowell Mills 12

Mirror 14

Queen of Heaven 16

No One Asks 18

Overseer 19

House Afire 20

Snow 21

Irish Need Not Apply 22

Astral 23

A Thin Place 25

Snow Globes 26

Sea 27

Spring 28

Selected Readings 29

for Mary Ward Brown

Announced by all the trumpets of the sky,
Arrives the snow, and, driving o'er the fields,
Seems nowhere to alight: the whited air
Hides hills and woods, the river, and the heaven,
And veils the farm-house at the garden's end.
The sled and traveler stopped, the courier's feet
Delayed, all friends shut out, the housemates sit
Around the radiant fireplace, enclosed
In a tumultuous privacy of storm.
from "The Snow Storm," Ralph Waldo Emerson

Introduction

Mary Paul was a real person, a New England farm girl who moved to Lowell, MA, to work in the textile mills during the middle of the 1800s. Like most, she lived in a boarding house, and, like most, she shared the conflicting feelings that beset them all regarding those they left behind: what it meant to be a proper young woman at that time—the need to do something more than survive, the drive to succeed, to see a wider world, to earn a living she could see and count, yet to be pious, ladylike, a good daughter, sister, to be, ultimately, marriageable.

But Mary had higher aspirations. She was influenced by the Romanticism of the time, she continued to educate herself beyond the village school as she worked, and ultimately, she moved to the longest-lived of all the utopian experiments of the 19th century, the North American Phalanx in New Jersey. She left that place only when it closed due to financial difficulties.

Even when she married the son of her former boarding house mother, she moved in interesting circles, times: he ultimately worked for Tiffany and Co. She seemed to understand she lived a more than ordinary life in extraordinary times, working on and publishing her family's history, including her own in careful detail. I am working here from about 30 letters to her father, Bela Paul, now archived in Vermont's historical society.

I have also created an Irish girl—I named her Brigid—based on extensive studies in secondary documents. Few Irish were hired to work inside the mills during the time New England girls were heavily recruited, though the men can be credited with the hard labor of trenching canals and building these factories. Later Irish immigrants would make up a large portion of the mill girls. Mary Paul herself seemed utterly unaware of the few immigrants around her during her time in Lowell.

All quoted material is from Mary's letters to her father Bela, archived in the Vermont Historical Society unless otherwise indicated. The chronology is sometimes altered in the interest of theme.

Rhyme

Mary, Mary,
Quite contrary,
How does your garden grow?

The constant knell
of the factory bells,
keeps the pretty maids
all in a row.

Counting
Mary Paul Considers Leaving Home

I made
the mill, counting,
measuring
corn rising,
snow falling, creeping
shadows, counting
all by inches. Counting
coins, stitches picked,
knitted, dropped,
apples, eggs gathered,
weeds plucked, invaders
among the neat
rows of our kitchen
garden.
Counting
days, girls, boys,
brothers
leaving.

I hexed my
convoluted brain
counting 'til all
it could conceive ticked.
The fuzzed bee
dropping in his line,
fat and sloppy,
his inconsistent hum
crowding then teasing
my vexed ear.

My hand against my heart,
its beating,
one and two and three
and four—Father's,
Henry's footsteps, counting
until all the world lines up
and I can go.

What I Want

Dear Father,
"I want
you to consent
to let me go."
"I want
you to think
of it and make
up your mind."

"If possible" I want
to go
to Lowell
or some place other
than "here."

No, I have not written
Mr. Angell. If only he would let
me talk, I could
convince him of his
error. Here
I cannot earn
what I can there.
I "need
clothes."

"I want
to see you
and to talk to you
about it." "If I could go
with some steady girl,"
like Mercy Jane,
"I might do well."

"Aunt Sarah gains
slowly."

Mary

Hens
    Mary on the Farm

I stood the feather
in the earth because, for luck,
my mother taught me to. What good,
I wondered. Chicken's, not crow's or
raven's: Hens scratch
at the dirt, stretching earthworms
until they snap, pecking at bugs,
or the table scraps we toss
them. How heavy they appear,
their lurching flight, their silly
cackling—a crowd of hens,
rooster. They think he brings
the day in when he crows
and the sun
rises.

Mother heard a hen crow
once at the barn door—unlucky. She took
its head. A young man died,
though, the next farm over,
and there were so few
of them.

And she died then
when I was just eleven.
I am as good as penned
here on this farm.
My father, crippled, cries,
when I ask to go,
"All things in their season,
and according to their nature."
I am freighted
with his care, waiting
for the feather's promise.

Shoes

Dear Father,
I want the
shoes
you made for me.

I dread the cold,
the wet and snow,
the ice. Last year, a girl slipped
upon the frozen path
and fell down dead. She "broke
her neck."

I worry about your lameness,
weary as I
am, the looms clattering,
like the horses' hooves
on the road coming
here.

I want my old shoes
to stand before the loom, to make
my bricked way home.
I think they will be large
enough.
Please send
them.

Mary

Lace

Dear Father,
"I am in the spinning
room"
where the dust flies
off the winding thread
like snow we have not seen
beyond these walls
this warm winter.

It settles on my lashes,
rims my eyes.
Against my damp skin
it is like the spider's web
I walk through and carry
away from the still woods,

or it is like the down
of the chickens we keep, clinging
to their just-laid eggs
steaming in the cold.

I wish it were lace—
a white veil
swept against my face,
a green aisle spinning
out before me.

The Bells

The bells, on Sunday, call
us to services.
We must attend.
Father, perhaps you would like
to know our rules, the bells:
half past four, wake up to work, at seven,
breakfast, then again at half past twelve,
dinner, seven, supper, at ten for sleep,
the bells.

They call, peal, ring, sing, clang
the perfect arc the sun marks
soundlessly. The heavy bells
Mama said knell. Time is new
here; the bells of the brides and births
and funerals are lifetime's time. Factory time
never quickens. We work; we work.
The machines go click and clack.
Ding dong is tick tock. The tolling bells
have made of me
a clock.

Somnambulism

They cannot know, here,
I am walking in my sleep.
Across the silent bodies
of my bedmates breathing out,
down the stairs, beyond the door, I
see that I am standing
barefoot in the icy street.
They would send me home.

When I was small, my mother found
me once, sleeping, curled
among the chickens
near their coop. Because their silly heads
were swallowed up in fluff,
their tiny shifty eyes shut,
I might have been the bad egg,
the savaged hen they'd shun
in light of day. "Chicken girl,"
my brothers called me.

I took to wearing small bells hung
upon a string around
my ankle, like for cows and cats, that is
the barely conscious,
molesters of fences,
and skulkers in the night.
We must be hung
with bells.

Mother says, perhaps I was
the cinder girl sleeping not in ashes, but
feathers, always craving warmth,
no shame in that.
I am no princess. This hard
life is no dream. I walk
towards something even
in my sleep.

Touch

Dear Father,
"I give my love to all
that would inquire
for me."

My mother died leaving me
in a house full of men. I miss her
more here among these girls
than when I was a sister
to three brothers. I miss her
touch.

Here we sometimes
wash each other's hair
in the kitchen by the fire,
strong soap, but warm water
and our fingers kneading
the clotting cotton dust
away. Suthera Griffith wept
once when her turn came.

Some here pay
the traveling bump men,
phrenologists they claim,
pretty men in shiny suits,
flattering and flirting, to read
them. "Amatos,"
they mutter, massaging that bulging bone
just above the skull's base—
"You are a woman rich in love
to give. And such abundance speaks
itself in all you do and say."
Our faces heat and color. Tomorrow,
we will bind our hair against
the hungry looms.

Peddlers

Dear Father,
Many intrude
when I would be writing
my letters or reading. These few
hours, our only leisure before
bed, the bell, the looms.

Have you partitioned your room?
This winter may be colder,
and your rheumatism?
I cannot help you.
Last week I had seven
with five for board. I bought
new overshoes. Next pay, a dollar
above my board. My health holds, though
last week I kept to bed
three days.

I heard from Bridgewater. Mrs. Angell
maligns me. "Mary Paul could find no work,"
she says and calls me lazy. I could not stay
in her service, Father. Mr. Angell—

The peddlers have come with
bits of things, fancy buttons
of shell and bone, tortoise combs
and pots of rouge, colors
against these acres of snow.
The ache of work is tomorrow's.

Yours,
Mary

At the Lowell Mills

Dear Mother,
For all I have
a name, I am
the Brigid. They
are no better. We
all come
from dead
farms, useless girls, no
one to marry
us.

When the potatoes rotted,
the plants'
leaves like tired flags,
our green world smelled
spoiled. Still,

Ireland has its sacred
places, no
matter that the crops failed.
There's starved and
there's starved.

At the holy well I
could lie down
in a boat of stone, a seep
of water at my back, the stream
chattering, old skirts ripped
to shreds and tatters
tied upon
the tree limbs—tiny ghosts,
pale fingers, hag's hair, fish feathers,
tongues wagging, fronds unfurling, Pray
for us St. Brigid.

But Brigid here keeps
her hair, her skirts, bound
away from the bite
of machines, herself
as well, and tight.

Mirror

Father, I waited
a long time
for your letter
of last Friday?
What am I doing?
I am in the spinning
room, tending four sets of warp,
one girl's work.

        I was obliged to give
        the ticket master a dollar
        as if my fare had not been paid?

        And Mrs. Angell gossips
        I am bad
        because I did not stay
        in her service.

But here the overseer says I am good,
and he will do right
by me.

At home I worked and never
saw the the profit of it
except that we got on.
But here the coins are in my hand.

The Griffith girls and I stayed up
last night and by candlelight
watched our faces
in the mirror.
Their mother says if evil
is near
its face will peer
over our shoulders,
will look back

at us.

Who am I?
A girl who no longer gives.
I cannot send money home
yet. I earn my board
and lodging, some left
for a few things I
need.

Queen of Heaven
Brigid at Prayer

I could have been dead
Irish, my bones
picked and drifting
at the bottom of the sea,
my body
dissolved in salty blue.

All you farm girls, you
Americans, packed
in your boardinghouse beds
like tinned fish. I prefer
our shanty, smelling
of sod and soaked boards,
of filthy men and puking babies,
of want.
Here at least smoke
perfumes the air. It chases
me around the room, a stream
of incense.

Puritan misses the priest calls you,
puffed up with your own
authority, afraid of rote and rosary,
of chant, of all the holy saints, one
for every misery.
I am Irish, nothing less
than you, for certain, before
this grand
and indifferent machine.

Intercede for me,
Mary, not you Mary Paul of the prim
smile, the back of you stiff
as a pole. Hail Mary, Queen
of Heaven, pray for me, the Brigid,
mother Mary

of earth and oceans,
treading on the serpent
and in your arms a King.

No One Asks

No one asks
if we are happy
here. Are we good? How
could it be
otherwise? Am I a good
custodian of my strict machine?
We get along
fine. I keep my hair tied
back, my apron neat. He bites; I
serve him. In other words, I
don't jam him up. He predictably
extrudes. All is good.

But am I good? How
could I be otherwise? I limp
along the walkway on stiff feet. I do not
swerve. The canals have the water
trained. I eat
when fed. I sleep flat
on my back between
two other industrial
goddesses.
It's not like we can toss
or turn. That is for our dreams. Sorry,
dear Father, for this old saw: we sleep
like the dead. And the dead
are always good. They have no
choice.

Overseer
Brigid Wonders

Would those be my
fingers you observe, sir?
Pale-skinned, knob-eyed, bloat
of a man—overseer. Keep watch
on the hands. See over my shoulder, not
the slope of my breast. It is my
quick touch you and yours like, spend
for, my eyes darting
within the scope of these
frames, cornered. I am a cog
in the rickety rack of your machinery,
except I feel
your hot breath on my cheek. I am
your factory girl. I know I smell
of sweat, yet you pull it all
in like a scent-starved dog. I am a piece
of all of us, women lined up across
the floor, bell-skirted for the ringing,
dripping in this stifling
heat. What would you have over
me? What looms in your man's mind?
A perfect yard of cloth is all? Irish come
cheap, you think. Touch me once, and I will
bite and you will suffer in the maw
of the machine I am. If we
are whores, I will never be yours.

House Afire

My mother taught me
to forgive and to get
along. Do as told, return
anger with love. Boys will be
boys, she said of my brothers, and
your father needs your respect and
obedience.

I was a good girl. My father made
shoes; my mother most everything
else. My father was paid in
coins and in bills; my mother with
a roof overhead, the pleasure
of our noisy, endless needs, our
needy company.

Every dawn the chickens squawked
for their corn, the pig squealed
for her slop. My father sat in noisy
silence demanding his mush and tea.

Then one morning, the house burned
down. How we all scattered and fled, saving
only our skins. Mother came through
last of all, in her arms a bucket holding last
night's cornbread and the quilt she was piecing
for the winter's coming.

We forgot our shoes. We stood
barefoot together in the smoking
yard, watching as everything burned right
down, sparks afloat on the hot
drafts, alive in the spell of our mother's screaming,
"House afire!"

Snow

This world is upside
down; the lint rises
like ash from a twisted
paper burning
in my hand.
First, we called it snow, frosting
our hair and faces, yet
its updrift flocks
the ceiling. Above us hangs
a gray and dimpled cloud
of fluff and fiber.

Dear Father,
Outside the winter's "very mild;"
"I have not seen a particle of snow."
Though they "tell me I am growing
very poor," spinning—
yet "I stand it well." And
"I was paid nine" bright
coins this last week.
It is getting dark. The bells
are quiet until the morning.
I can drift
to sleep and dream of snow
flying there at home, whitening
the holly but for the berries' burn.

If it is cold, tomorrow
I will not wear my black
alpaca to the mill, my best,
and right for such a season.

Irish Need Not Apply
What Brigid Knows

Irish need not apply
themselves to subtle thoughts,
to contemplation of anything beyond
the rot of the potato, the luck
of landing within the largesse
of this America. I and my kind
are saved by a country who needs but
does not love us. I and my Pope. Boo!
We frighten you former Pilgrims sailing your furious
little boats across the same gray sea, starving,
and sweating, and bickering your way
away from a church become too rich
and powerful, a piety factory for the making
of the complacent and conforming. Non-
conformists you are, holding that we of the nasty
shanties, muddied streets, of men drunken and violent
and squalling dirty babies live outside
your precious grace. You are so clean
and so earnest. You are so smug in your own
salvation. We Catholics, we Irish take this
in, it is our new communion. I stand
beside you, Mary Paul. I work
as well as you. Look at me; speak
to me, just once. I am here
so that you may rise. We Irish, we superstitious
Papists, we are your stairway, kneeling
like stair steps before our altars. At least, when we conform,
it is not to a cold machine and the greed
of men?

Astral

> *Mary S. Paul was "a sympathizer with the ideas of Theodore Parker, when his followers were few." (Stiles Genealogy, Vermont Historical Society)*

Mr. Parker speaks of our being
two, of God housed
in our bodies.

The manager's wife
looks out
upon these bricked
towers, brimming
with hive-life, her mansion lit
with astral lamps
like the one—
its crystals shivering—
in the window. We watch
from below, this, our only
star.

Yet we desire
a life beyond
the sealed windows
of the mill, we hang
our poems, stories, picture
post cards and the sun
shines through them. Illuminated,
words we can say
by heart.

The machines drive
us, our hands serve
them, our hearts beat
to their gray, insistent gathering
of fiber, thread, and all
the world's peace
and quiet.
Still, something in us aspires
to a farther mansion—
so we go astral,
our Eden, the green
source, just the hills, the trees
out there through the scrim
of window words.

A Thin Place

Abby and I sleep
at the top of this house,
four stories high—
one or two rooms deep.

Ours is a thin place,
between us and the storms
a mere roof. We "feared
it would blow off last
night."

Raised up in the sky above
the new trees
we stoke our hired stove
and the damp dark flies
to the window panes
kinned to what's outside.

Mr. Parker preaches the great
soul, within us all, is rising
like heat from the burning
wood, like the jarring bells become
soft and musical as they wake
us before dawn, like the constant roar
below is a murmur, just
a whispering now, my mother's breath
against my ear.

Abby and I are pressed
against the sky here,
our spirits to that vast
one, as close as close
can be. We give up
our ghostlier selves,
our weary bodies sinking
into sleep.

Snow Globe

Outside the glass, the trees turn
bright, as if, once the nights
lengthen, they must light
the dusk, the dawn.

In here, if you could see
into the high-
up windows, you would not
hear the thrashing looms
or know how dry
the floating, wooly snow-
fall, or see it does not
melt away.

"Enchanting," you
might say,
the pretty girls,
their hands dancing,
the hushed snow fly, held
in a globe, trembling
as if shaken.

Sea

Blue, like the robin's egg
the traveller says, but
brighter, the whole sea, south,
south, south of here, where the land
ends, Florida—and brighter
as the sun lights
it.

Rare, here, this greeny blue—
the fragment of a broken
egg, crushed in the grass, seas
of grass, blue
sky, the pinks and reds
of blossoms, apples
ripening, fading purple—
lady slippers, violets.

My dresses are drab.
We cannot make
the colors. I pinch them
into my cheeks, a blush
that dims, the flicker of rose
in a flame.

My grandmother or great
or great crossed the Atlantic.
My eyes are blue, a fragment
of sea, passed down,
remembered.

Spring
    A Found Poem, March, 1855

"I have a glass
of water, buds
of the mayflower
which I got in the woods
the 21st of Feb,
doesn't that sound like
Spring?"

Selected Reading

Dublin, Thomas. *Women at Work: The Transformation of Work and Community in Lowell, Massachusetts, 1826-1860.* 2nd edition. New York: Columbia UP, 1993.

The Lowell Offering: Writings by New England Mill Women (1840-1845). Ed. Benita Eisler. New York: Harper & Row, 1977.

Mitchell, Brian C. *The Paddy Camps: The Irish of Lowell, 1821-61.* Urbana: U of Illinois P, 1988.

Moran, William. *The Belles of New England: The Women of the Textile Mills and the Families Whose Wealth They Wove.* New York: Thomas Duane, St. Martin's P, 2002.

Robinson, Harriet H. *Loom & Spindle or Life Among the Early Mill Girls.* Kailua, HI: Pacifica P, 1976.

No, **Susie Paul** is not related to Mary Paul. This collection of poems about a Lowell, MA, textile mill worker has its deepest roots in her father Marvin Paul's sense of adventure. While he worked for Raytheon near Boston, and before the family traveled to the Mississippi Coast where he was to prepare for the opening of NASA's newest operation—now Stennis Space Center, they made a pilgrimage to Plymouth, MA. There they visited a mock Colonial village and a replica of the Mayflower and were surprised as are all by the tiny size of the famous rock. Nevertheless, she was enraptured.

Though she specialized in 20th-century America in her doctoral program at the University of South Carolina, her favorite periods to teach were the Colonial and the 19th century in America. At a crossroads regarding the personal revelations required of lyric poetry and influenced by Andrew Hudgins' collection, *After the Lost War* about the poet Sydney Lanier, she contemplated writing through the voices of historical figures instead.

In a moment of serendipity, she stumbled across a book about the women of Fairhope, AL, a utopian community, while browsing in the local flea market. One of these women had worked as a girl in Lowell, and Mary Paul's letters were mentioned by the scholar/author in his bibliography. After the loan of these by the Vermont Historical Society, Mary Paul's journey and her complex feelings found their way into poetry

Susie Paul has taught for roughly 45 years, at every level from ninth graders to graduate students. She is the mother of Amelia Johnson, B.A. Kenyon College and M.A. Harvard; an educator, and Joseph Johnson, a gifted musician and cook. Both work and live in Birmingham, AL. Their dad, Gene, their stepmom, Cheryl, and Paul raised them together and are so proud of the people they have become.

As their mom used to irritate them by repeating lines of poems she was working on, ceaselessly sometimes, they are proud of their mom and her book, perhaps a bit relieved, too.

At present Paul is at work on a new collection based on the life of Marie Howland, the Fairhope woman she discovered in the small book from the flea market where she first found Mary Paul. She is supported in this project by a grant from Alabama's Bicentennial Committee.

www.ingramcontent.com/pod-product-compliance
Lightning Source LLC
LaVergne TN
LVHW041504070426
835507LV00012B/1317